True Survival

MICHAEL BENSON

TRAPPED IN A VOLCANO

Virginia Loh-Hagan

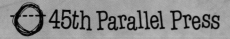
45th Parallel Press

Published in the United States of America by Cherry Lake Publishing
Ann Arbor, Michigan
www.cherrylakepublishing.com

Reading Adviser: Marla Conn MS, Ed., Literacy specialist, Read-Ability, Inc.
Book Cover Design: Felicia Macheske

Photo Credits: ©Alexey Kamenskiy/Shutterstock.com, cover; ©sculpies/Shutterstock.com, 5; ©gnoparus/
Shutterstock.com, 7; ©Eachat/iStock.com, 8; ©Alexander Demyanenko/Shutterstock.com, 11; ©Bryan Busovicki/
Shutterstock.com, 12; ©Jaromir Chalabala/Shutterstock.com, 14; ©robert cicchetti/Shutterstock.com, 17;
©nicehelix/Shutterstock.com, 19; ©Keith Levit/Shutterstock.com, 20; ©Jaromir Chalabala/Shutterstock.com, 23;
©photocagiao/Shutterstock.com, 24; ©sfam_photo/Shutterstock.com, 27; ©Makushin Alexey/Shutterstock.com, 29

Graphic Elements Throughout: ©Gordan/Shutterstock.com; ©adike/Shutterstock.com; ©Yure/Shutterstock.com

45th Parallel Press is an imprint of Cherry Lake Publishing.

Library of Congress Cataloging-in-Publication Data has been filed and is available at catalog.loc.gov

Cherry Lake Publishing would like to acknowledge the work of The Partnership for 21st Century Skills.
Please visit *www.p21.org* for more information.

Printed in the United States of America
Corporate Graphics

table of contents

chapter one

Movie Men

Who is Michael Benson? Who is Christopher Duddy? Who is Craig Hosking? What are volcanoes?

Michael Benson is part of the Hollywood crowd. Hollywood is in Los Angeles, California. It's a famous place. Movies are made there.

Benson is a director of photography. He's a movie **cameraman**. Cameramen operate cameras. They make movies. They make television shows. They capture moving images. They use many cameras. They move cameras around. They get the best shots.

They work in **studios**. Studios are places designed to make movies. Cameramen also work on **location**. This means they travel. They film at specific places. They work all kinds of hours.

Cameramen work with directors and actors.

spotlight biography

Ludger Sylbaris lived in Saint-Pierre, Martinique. Martinique is an island in the West Indies. Sylbaris was a criminal. He was taken to jail. This happened in 1902. Sylbaris's cell was small. It was underground. It had no windows. It had a small slit in the door. This cell saved his life. Mount Pelée volcano erupted. It destroyed Saint-Pierre. Buildings were burned down. People were burned to death. Over 30,000 people died. The city burned for several days. Sylbaris was found 4 days after the eruption. He was trapped in his cell. He peed on his clothes. He covered his face. He stuffed his clothes in the slit. But his cell still got hot. He was burned by the air. But he survived. He was pardoned for his crimes. He was hired by a famous circus. He was the first black man in the show. He died in 1929 of natural causes.

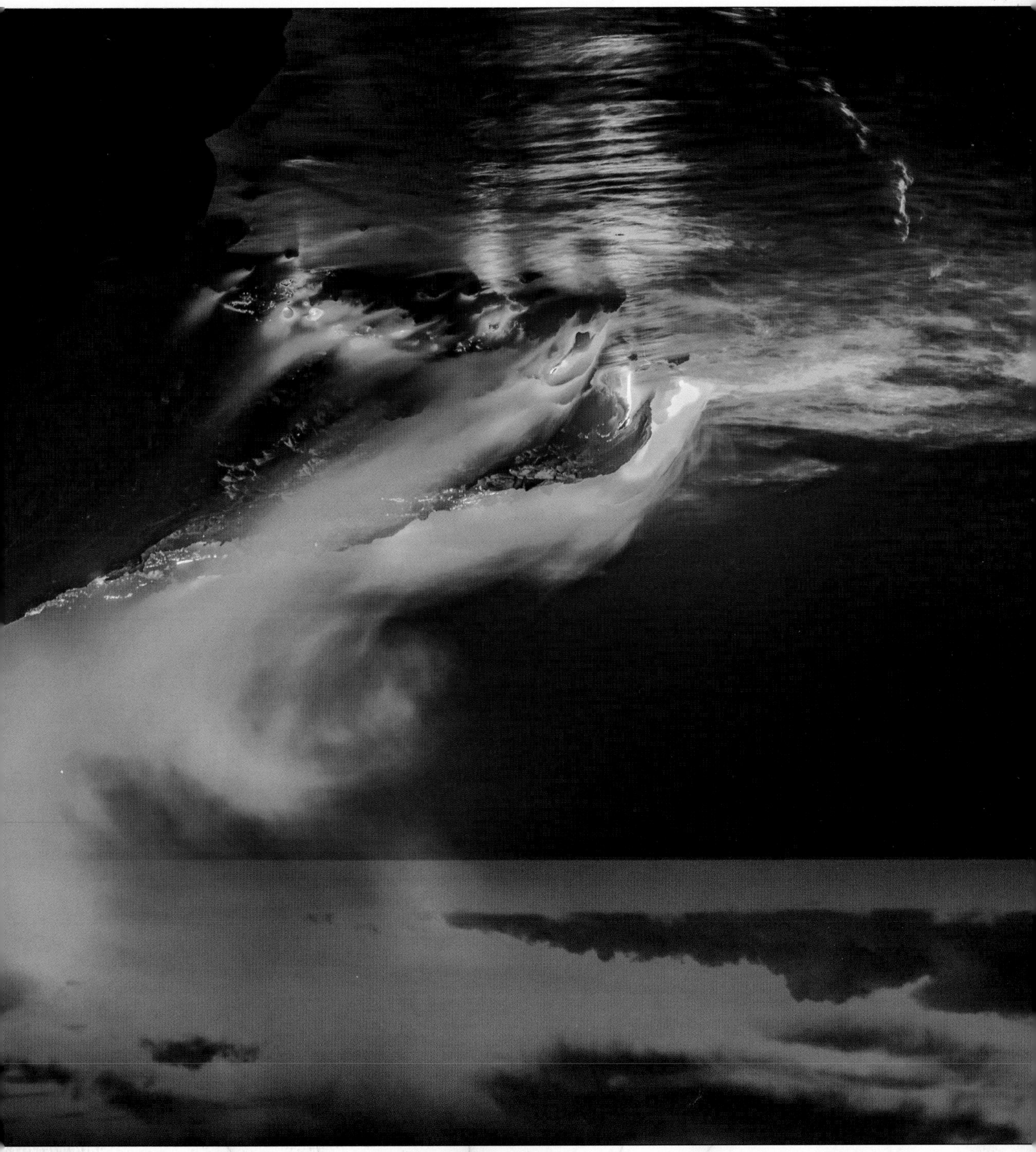

Helicopters can fly to places that planes can't get to.

Benson is known for doing good work. He's worked on many popular movies. He worked on *Terminator 2*. He worked on *Ghost*. He worked on *Patriot Games*.

Christopher Duddy is a camera **technician**. Technicians work with equipment. They help cameramen. They clean cameras. They fix cameras. They operate cameras.

Craig Hosking is a **licensed** helicopter pilot. Licenses are special permits. Hosking got his license at age 16. He was the youngest pilot to do this. He works for the movies. He does **aerial** work. Aerial means from the air. Hosking takes cameramen to locations. He helps film things from the air.

Paramount Pictures is a big company. It makes movies. It hired Benson, Duddy, and Hosking to work on *Sliver*. *Sliver* is a mystery movie. This happened in 1992.

Benson, Duddy, and Hosking were hired to film **volcano eruptions**. Volcanoes are openings in the Earth's surface. Eruptions are explosions. Some volcanoes are active. They let out ash, gas, and hot **magma**. Magma is hot liquid rock under the Earth's surface. It's called **lava** when it comes out.

Hosking flew Benson and Duddy to a volcano named Kilauea. Kilauea is in Hawaii. It's one of the most active volcanoes. It's been erupting since 1983. It's the home of Pele. Pele is the Hawaiian goddess of fire and volcanoes.

◄ Kilauea is a Hawaiian name. It means "much spreading" or "spewing."

chapter two

Crash and Burn

What happened to Hosking's helicopter? What happened to Benson, Duddy, and Hosking? How did Hosking get saved?

Benson, Duddy, and Hosking wanted to film the smoke and lava. There was no active lava flow. But there was a pool of lava. It glowed. It came from a deep pit by the **crater**. Craters are at the tops of volcanoes. They look like bowls.

Hosking's helicopter had two cameras. Hosking flew over the crater. He followed Hawaiian tradition. He gave Pele a special gift. He wanted to make Pele happy. He gave her a bottle. He threw it in the crater. But he missed. His bottle landed near the crater wall. It didn't go in the fire pit. This wasn't a good sign.

Volcanoes are dangerous. But they're also beautiful.

The helicopter was about 10 feet (3 meters) above the crater's floor. Smoke was rising. It made it hard to see. Hosking had a hard time flying the helicopter. He lost power. He yelled, "We've got a problem."

Benson and Duddy looked up. They saw the volcano wall. Duddy said, "We're dead!" Benson saw the helicopter blades hit the wall. The blades came off. The helicopter crashed to the ground. It broke apart in three pieces.

All three men fell inside the volcano crater. They barely missed the boiling lava pool. They fell in a pocket of fresh air. They weren't hurt.

Ash can damage plane engines.

explained by science

Volcanoes affect people in many ways. Most lava flows are slow. They're too slow to run over moving people. But they can run over buildings and roads. Pyroclastic flows are special. They move quickly. They run over people. They're deadly. They're very hot. They cause people to explode. Volcanoes can also cover towns in ash. Ash is heavy. It causes buildings to fall. Volcano gases are most dangerous closest to the opening. They're less dangerous farther away. Air mixes in and spreads the bad gases. The gases are really bad for people with breathing problems. They cause lung problems. They cause headaches. They cause eyes to bleed. Being around gases for a long time is bad. But being around gases for a short time is okay. Volcanoes also help people. They make rich soil. These soils can be used for farming.

None of the men could see each other. There was too much smoke. Duddy and Benson tried to climb out. They kept slipping. They kept grabbing crumbling rock. Benson was about 75 feet (23 m) below the rim. Duddy was about 30 feet (9 m) higher. They were both stuck on ledges. Hosking was near the top. He was able to fix his radio. He called for help.

Two hours later, a rescue helicopter came. The rescuers found Hosking. They saw him through a break in the clouds. They lifted him to safety. They couldn't see Duddy and Benson. But they couldn't climb down to find them. This was too risky.

◄ Rescue workers are trained to help people.

chapter three

Fire Trap

How did Duddy escape? What happened to Benson in the volcano?

Benson and Duddy heard the helicopter. They yelled for help. Rescuers could hear their shouts. But they couldn't help. There was heavy rain. There was fog. There was smoke and steam. This created a "**whiteout**." The rescuers couldn't see anything. They could only see a few feet ahead of them.

It was getting dark. Benson and Duddy were stuck. They clung to their ledges.

Once an hour, a rescuer blew a whistle. Benson said, "It was the greatest feeling in the world to hear that whistle." The whistle kept his hopes up.

Clouds of ash and gases come out of volcanoes.

would you?

- **Would you visit a volcano?** Over 100 million people visit volcanoes each year. Chances of being killed by a volcano are small. People shouldn't visit high-risk zones. They should be prepared. They should limit their time at volcanoes. But there are no promises. Things could happen.

- **Would you want to be a cameraman?** There are two types of cameramen. One type works in studios. They can practice. They have time to get the perfect shot. They meet TV or movie stars. Another type works in news. They record things live. They have one chance. They must work fast.

- **Would you rather be trapped in a volcano or in ice?** Volcanoes are really hot. People get burned. They breathe in poisons. Ice is really cold. People can get frostbite. They can freeze to death.

Benson could hear the lava moving and popping. He said, "At night, it was like a light show. The lava sounded like surf pounding against the shore."

Benson and Duddy survived the first night. Duddy said, "There were several times when I just gave in to the fact that I was going to die." But he didn't quit. He started climbing. He got to the top. He was safe.

But Benson was still stuck. He heard something fall. He thought Duddy had fallen and died.

There was a lake of lava below Benson.

CAUTION

AVOID THE STEAM PLUME — IT IS HAZARDOUS TO YOUR HEALTH AND MAY BE LIFE-THREATENING

The plume contains hydrochloric acid and volcanic glass particles which can irritate eyes and skin and cause respiratory distress.

Benson thought he was in a movie. He said, "I was waiting for the director to say, 'Cut!' This is not a movie. This is real. And I'm actually sitting here, dying."

Benson was trapped another night. He couldn't sleep. He started seeing things. He started hearing things. His mind played tricks on him. He thought he saw his family. He thought he saw Pele. Pele appeared in front of him. He said, "I told her that she was not going to take me. I actually got up and screamed that at her."

◄ Volcano gases can affect people's minds and bodies.

chapter four

Out of the Ashes

How was Benson saved? Who is Tom Hauptman?

Benson waited for help. When it rained, he cupped his hands. He collected rainwater. He drank it. He prayed. He said the alphabet backward. He did things to keep busy. He did things to not go crazy. He hadn't slept. He hadn't eaten. He was at his breaking point.

The weather got better. The smoke started to clear. Tom Hauptman flew the rescue helicopter. He finally was able to see Benson. He flew into the crater. He dropped down a net. The net was a basket shaped like a chair. The net was attached to a long **cable**. Cables are strong ropes.

The rescue was extremely dangerous.

Hauptman fished Benson out.

Hauptman held the helicopter steady. He tried to get it closer to Benson. He threw the net out several times. The fog was coming back. So, Hauptman had to hurry.

Finally, Benson was able to catch the net. He grabbed hold. He climbed in. Hauptman pulled Benson out of the volcano.

Benson said, "They lifted me out of there and gave me the ride of my life." Then, he looked down. He yelled at Pele. He said, "You didn't beat me. You didn't get me."

survival tips

VOLCANO EXPLOSION!

- Stay away from active volcanoes. Stay away from lava.

- Be aware of rising water. Stay away from mudflows. Move up slope as quickly as possible.

- Stay away from flying rocks. Roll into a ball. Protect your head.

- Keep gas and ash away from your nose, ears, and mouth. Wear goggles. Wear a mask. Hold damp cloths over your face.

- Be ready to move. Leave the area. Listen to officials.

- Avoid ash. Keep skin covered. Wear long pants. Wear long sleeves.

- Find someplace to hide indoors. Seal windows and doors. Turn off fans. Turn off machines that bring in outside air.

- Check the area to make sure it's safe. Call for help. Take care of injuries.

chapter five

Happy Ending

What were Benson, Duddy, and Hosking treated for? What happened to the movie?

Jeffrey Judd is a park ranger. He was on the rescue helicopter. He said, "[Hauptman] knew we were hovering over Benson. So, we put the net down and let him get in blindly. We never saw him in the steam. But the rope went tight and there he was."

Hauptman flew Benson to the hospital. Benson said, "I'm feeling pretty good. I just have some lung problems because of the gases." His lungs were swollen. His throat was very sore. He lost his voice. His body lost water. He got sick from all the gases.

Duddy and Hosking also had lung and eye problems.